GOOD GIFTS

ONE YEAR IN THE
HEART OF A HOME

Good Gifts

ONE YEAR IN THE
HEART OF A HOME

KATHIE LEE GIFFORD

KATHIE'S KIDS, LLC.   OLD GREENWICH, CT

This book is dedicated to my family, here and gone, but never forgotten.

And to each friend, new and old, who has brought joy and comfort and

encouragement with them each time they came through our door.

I thank my God on every remembrance of them.

Foreword

CHANGE. It's a thrilling word to some and a terrifying word to others. But when we stop to think about it, we're all in a constant state of change: The clock changes every second, the tides, every six hours, seasons every three months and our bodies, aging one day at a time until our days on this earth pass away. So change is natural, then, right? And if it's natural, it's good. Right?

But change is not always for the better, is it? The loss of a loved one, a frightening diagnosis, a terrifying storm that leaves chaos and destruction in its wake or a husband or wife that leaves for a new partner. The illness of a beloved child. This kind of change is devastating but inevitable because we live in an imperfect world. So little is under our control that at times it can be maddening. So how do we survive the painful, destructive seasons in our lives? How do we weather the storms that bash our souls against the cliffs? Scripture tells us in Matthew 7:25: *"The rain came down, the streams rose, and the winds blew and beat against that house; yet it did not fall, because it had its foundation on the rock."*

I have based my very life on the truth of God's word and every day I try to walk the ancient paths that lead to wisdom: *"Show me your ways, Lord, and teach me your paths, guide me in your truth and teach me for you are my Saviour God and I hope in you all the day long."* (Psalm 25:4-5) As life around me changes, I cling to the One who never changes from everlasting to everlasting. The Eternal One.

I offer this book up as evidence of His unfailing love to me and my family, year after year, with a prayer that you, too, will find joy and comfort and hope for your life as well. God's promises are true. His love is real. Come: *"Taste and see that the Lord is good."* (Psalm 34:8)

Introduction

When you're young you never think that someday you're going to be 60 so then when it actually does happen to you you're simply stunned, which is ridiculous because you've had six decades to prepare for it! In my heart of hearts, I feel like I'm 28, but my thighs tell a different story. So I ignore my thighs and everything else that's fallen apart and I try to stay creative. I really do think that's one of the keys to happiness: Keep doing what makes you happy, keep impacting lives and keep creating something beautiful so you won't be tempted to fixate on your face!

And keep laughing. On August 16, 2013, I turned 60 and Frank turned 83. We couldn't believe it. As I often do, I looked at Frank and said, "Wow, I never thought you'd live this long." And as usual we laughed our butts off.

Our friends insisted that we celebrate this milestone so we pitched a tent, sent out some invites and gathered around for a crab feast with a country music band. It was awesome, and the perfect beginning to a very special year in our family's history: Our 20th year in the house on the cliff: GIFFT CLIFF.

This book celebrates God's faithfulness to our family. It celebrates His unfailing love to us and all who have ever come through our door. It celebrates all that is good about life and love and friendship and faith. And, oh, yes—FOOD!

Thank you for joining us for a special year in the heart of a home. Our home. And may God bless you and your family, too.

August

JOYFUL IS THE PERSON WHO FINDS WISDOM,
THE ONE WHO GAINS UNDERSTANDING.
FOR WISDOM IS MORE PROFITABLE THAN SILVER
AND HER WAGES ARE BETTER THAN GOLD.
WISDOM IS MORE PRECIOUS THAN RUBIES;
NOTHING YOU DESIRE CAN COMPARE WITH HER.

Proverbs 3:13-15

FOR I WILL BE LIKE AN OLIVE TREE, FLOURISHING
IN THE HOUSE OF GOD AND TRUSTING
IN HIS UNFAILING LOVE FOREVER AND EVER.

Psalm 58:2

August

Frank and I couldn't afford our house when we bought it twenty years ago and we certainly couldn't afford it if we were trying to buy it today.

It was, and is, a gift. I can hear you exclaiming now, "You mean someone *gave* it to you? For free?"

No, but when we fell in love with this 1920's Mediterranean home on the Long Island Sound in Connecticut, it was on the market for way more than we could afford. So we prayed. I prayed more than Frank. He kept saying, "Don't get your hopes up, Honey. There's already an offer on it from some Wall Street guy and I don't want you to get your heart broken when we make our best offer."

But from the moment we drove up the stone driveway, I knew. I just knew that the Lord had a plan for us right there. That we would build our family there and turn that house into a home that would honor Him.

So we made a very low offer, saying, "It's all we have but we love the house and you don't need to change a thing to it. Here's our money and we can close in thirty days."

Then we held our breath. Three days later the realtor called us and said, "Cody has a cannon." Instantly we remembered the pre-civil war cannon at the end of the property. "The house is yours," he said. Frank and I just marveled that such a miracle had happened.

The Gifford family moved in on August 2, 1994, our daughter Cassidy's first birthday, and we are celebrating twenty years of life and loss and growth and pain and joy and sorrow and dreams this very year.

So, then, I know you're wondering, "How was the house a gift?"

It turns out that the man who sold us the house had attended a Pro Am tennis tournament years before. When he tried to sign in he was informed that there was no record of his name on the attendee list. This very accomplished man was embarrassed, until Frank, sensing his discomfort, walked right up to him and said, "Hi, I'm Frank Gifford. I want you to play with me today!"

Instantly the situation *changed*. He went from the Odd Man Out to the Big Guy In! He had been a lifelong Giants fan, but Frank didn't know that at the time. He just knew he could make a difference in someone's life by being kind, right there, right then.

Later, when the realtor asked the man why we won the bid on his house he simply answered, "I want Frank Gifford to have my house."

He probably lost a fortune on the sale, but that didn't seem to bother him one bit. Some things aren't about money. And this book is one of them. All profits from the sales of *GOOD GIFTS* will benefit The Salvation Army.

EVERY GOOD AND PERFECT GIFT COMES FROM ABOVE,
STREAMING DOWN FROM THE FATHER
IN THE HEAVENLY REALMS WHO DOES NOT CHANGE
LIKE SHIFTING SHADOWS.

James 1:17

SUFFER THE LITTLE CHILDREN
AND FORBID THEM NOT,
TO COME UNTO ME:
FOR OF SUCH IS THE
KINGDOM OF HEAVEN.

Matthew 19:14

First day at home & Cassidy's First Birthday

August 2, 1994

Isabella & Julia, with Cody

*I*n the early 90's on a trip to Colorado, a handsome young man named Andy Medina met us at the airport. Frank and I immediately warmed to this sweet-natured, polite, and intelligent reservations director for Cordillera, the beautiful mountaintop resort 8600 feet high in the sky. During the two-hour long trip to Cordillera, Andy told us about Elvia Romo, the lovely Mexican girl he had fallen in love with and was hoping to marry. He proudly showed us the ring he had purchased and as he dropped us off, we wished him and Elvia a lifetime of happiness together.

None of us had any idea that Andy and Elvia would someday become members of our own family. But eventually they moved to Connecticut to help us manage our busy lives here. Their precious daughters, Julia and Isabella, were born, and Frank and I have loved them like our own grandchildren.

We are beyond blessed to have had this family in our lives for over twenty years. I'm convinced that Cody and Cassidy come home as often as they do, not to see Frank and me so much, but to see their beloved "little sisters."

Andy has become an incredible cook and landscaper through the years and he and Elvia have contributed many of the recipes contained in this book.

But what this family has contributed to the joy in our household is priceless.

Andy's Frutti de Mare

Ingredients

- 1 - 16 oz box linguine
- 1¼ cup extra virgin olive oil
- 6 whole garlic heads, finely chopped
- 3 tbsp unsalted butter
- 1 - 8 oz bottle of clam juice
- 1 cup fresh finely chopped parsley, set aside 2 tbsp for garnish

- 2 dozen medium size little neck clams
- aluminum foil
- ¾ lb rock shrimp or squid clean and deveined
- 5 lbs manila clams or cockles, thoroughly cleaned
- 4 plum tomatoes, seeded and coarsely chopped
- ½ cup white wine
- salt and pepper to taste

Directions

1. Cook linguine as directed and set aside.

2. In a large, deep roasting pan (can be cooked on 2 burners of stovetop or on an outdoor grill), heat pan to medium heat and add olive oil. Heat 2-3 mins.

3. Add garlic, stirring frequently until aroma begins to release (careful not to burn).

4. Add 2 tbsp of butter and melt, stirring frequently.

5. Add clam juice and salt and pepper to taste, incorporate, and bring to a boil.

6. Add ⅓ cup of parsley and stir.

7. Add little neck clams into the pan over the heat and cover with foil. Cook for 3-5 minutes until clams begin to open. These will take longer than the Manila clams and shrimp. Stir them around to give equal cooking time.

8. Add shrimp to center of pan and cook for 2-3 mins, covered.

9. With a slotted spoon, stir all clams and shrimp, and add remaining Manila clams. Cover and cook for another 8-10 min. When all clams have begun to open, add tomatoes and remaining parsley. Stir to incorporate all ingredients, cover, and cook for another 2-3 min. Then remove from heat.

10. In a separate sauce pan, add 2 cups of broth from clams and bring to a boil. Add remaining butter, wine and salt and pepper to taste. Reduce heat and simmer until mixture has reduced to half. On larger platter place linguini first and seafood mixture on top. Pour reduced sauce over top, sprinkle with remaining parsley, and serve immediately.

*W*e never seem to stop celebrating birthdays in August. No sooner have we licked the icing off our fingers after our dear friend Christine's July 30th birthday, then Cassidy's blowing out the candles on her cake on August 2nd. Now Hoda's a member of the family so we celebrate hers on August 9th. Then Frank's and mine on August 16th, and Andy's a day later on the 17th.

Leave it to Regis to take us out with a bang on August 25th.

I think we should just put up a big tent for the whole month and take it down after Labor Day!

This year, on August 2nd, 2014, we celebrated Cassidy's 21st birthday and the 20th anniversary of living in our house. We raised children and we built a home. We've weathered many storms and celebrated many milestones. We've laughed, and we've cried. We've buried my precious Daddy, watched the young people in our extended family marry, and we are looking forward to the birth of four new babies in the fall. Frank is about to become a great-grandfather for the first time and we couldn't be more grateful. Each day of each year is precious and now that we are running out of them, we're more aware than ever of each "good and perfect gift." And we're more in awe than ever of the gracious God who provides them.

Seek first the Kingdom of God and His righteousness. And all these things shall be added unto you.

Matthew 6:33

Amen!

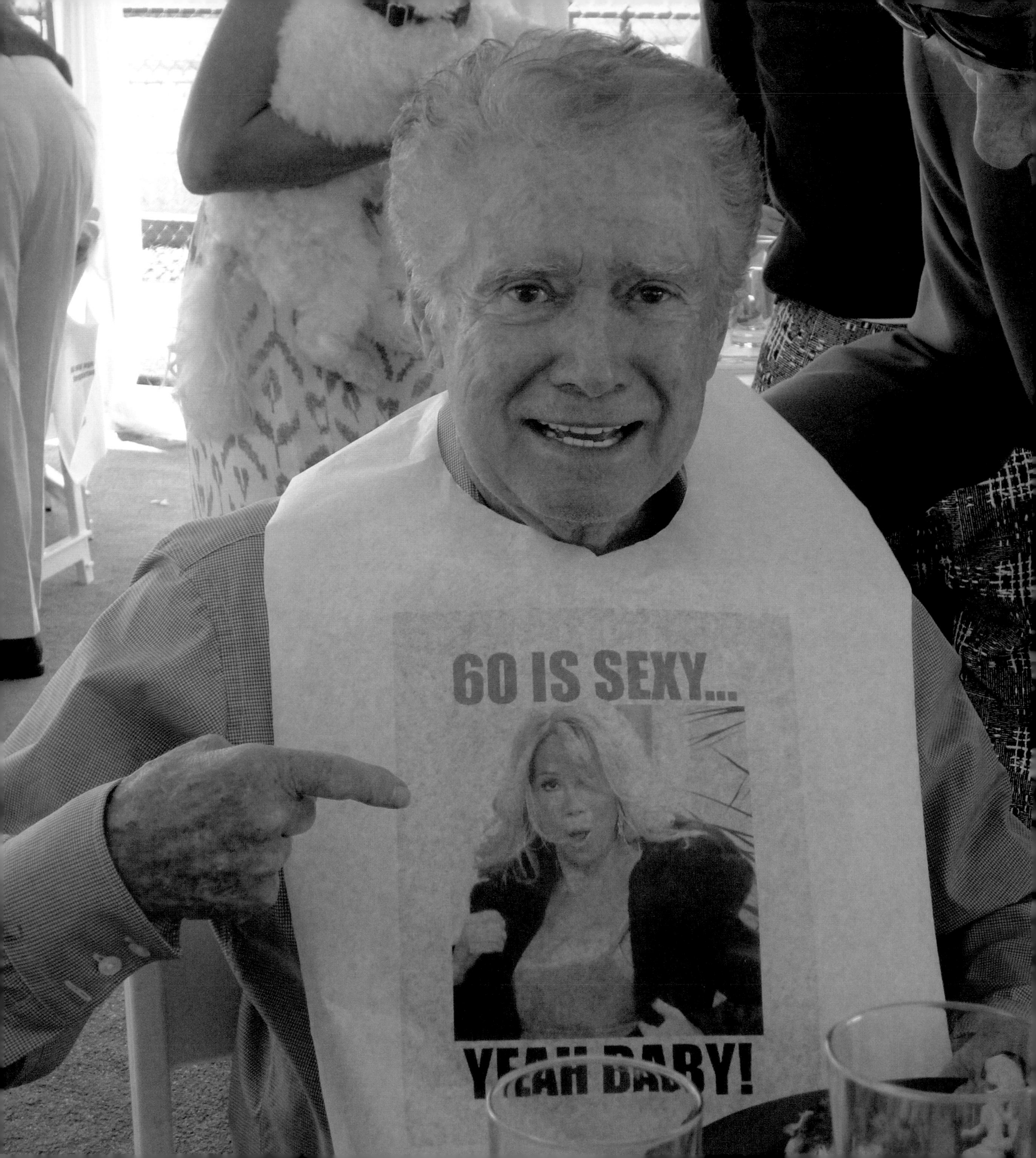
60 IS SEXY...
YEAH BABY!

*T*urning sixty was tougher than turning fifty which was tougher than turning forty which was—well, you get the picture.

But it certainly makes it easier when you share these milestones with people you love. People you trust. People who are there for you now because they've always been there for you before. People who have made your life the rich tapestry that it is today.

When we started our journey in this home I was almost 41 years old and deeply grateful for a husband and son I loved, a brand new daughter I adored, and a family and friends I wouldn't have traded for the world. I'm still that woman. Just more grateful and a few pounds heavier. And a few more years closer to my real home.

AS A FATHER HAS COMPASSION ON HIS CHILDREN,
SO THE LORD HAS COMPASSION ON THOSE WHO FEAR HIM;
FOR HE KNOWS HOW WE ARE FORMED,
HE REMEMBERS THAT WE ARE DUST.

Psalm 103:28

Happy Birthday
Kathie & Frank

Crabbie

Cake by Sweet Lisa's, Cos Cob, CT

Cassidy and "Boo Boo" Fuscone, best friends since forever!

It was the party that wouldn't end — and we didn't want it to!

September

THE EARTH IS THE LORD'S AND EVERYTHING IN IT.
FOR HE LAID THE EARTH'S FOUNDATION ON THE SEAS
AND BUILT ON THE OCEAN DEPTHS.

Psalm 24:1-10

September

September is the best kept secret in Connecticut and one of my favorite months. The weather is usually wonderful, the boats are still busy on the Sound and the water temperature is finally just right. People everywhere are trying to stuff as much of summer as they can into the remaining days they have. It's a race against time, of course, and one you can't win. But there is a sweetness in the air that permeates everything.

AS THE HEAVENS ARE HIGHER THAN THE EARTH,
SO ARE MY WAYS HIGHER THAN YOUR WAYS AND MY
THOUGHTS HIGHER THAN YOUR THOUGHTS.

Isaiah 55:9

Grilled Salmon Fillet with sun dried tomato topping

makes 4 servings

Ingredients

- 4 salmon fillets with skin on (6 oz portions)
- ¾ cup sun dried tomatoes, finely chopped
- 2 tbsp unsalted butter, softened
- 2 tbsp grapeseed oil
- 1 tbsp Mrs. Dash original blend seasoning
- Pam cooking spray for high temp cooking
- aluminum foil

Directions

1. Remove salmon fillets from refrigerator and allow to come to room temperature.

2. Make topping: In a small bowl, combine sun dried tomatoes and butter. Mix thoroughly and set aside.

3. Preheat grill or cast iron griddle to medium heat. Brush fillets with grapeseed oil and season with *Mrs. Dash* seasoning.

4. Generously spray cooking surface with cooking spray. Place fillets on the grill, skin side up. Grill side without skin for approximately 2-3 minutes, watching carefully not to burn.

5. Flip to skin-down side and grill for 3-4 minutes. Cover with foil until skin is crispy.

6. Preheat oven to 375 degrees. Place generous portion of sun dried tomato topping on top of fillets. Heat for another 6-7 minutes, until sun dried tomatoes begin to crisp.

7. Serve immediately.

Lunch at Lola's Lookout, September 2013

Shrimp Scampi

Ingredients

- 1 - 16 oz box linguine
- 1½ pounds large shrimp, peeled and deveined.
- 4 tbsp olive oil
- ¼ cup unsalted butter, softened
- 4 cloves garlic, minced
- 2 pinches red pepper flakes
- ½ cup white wine
- 1 large lemon, juiced
- ¼ cup curly parsley leaves, stems removed and finely chopped. Set aside 2 tbsp for garnish.
- fresh ground salt and pepper to taste

Directions

1. Cook pasta according to directions.

2. Rinse shrimp and pat dry.

3. Heat a large skillet over medium high heat. Add olive oil, 2 tbsp of butter, and melt.

4. Add minced garlic and red pepper flakes. Sauté, stirring frequently until aroma releases, for 2-3 minutes. Be careful not to burn!

5. Add shrimp and season with fresh ground salt and pepper. Sauté until shrimp begins to turn pink, about 1-2 minutes. Then flip shrimp and cook an additional 1-2 minutes.

6. Remove shrimp from pan and set aside and keep warm.

7. Add wine, lemon, and remaining butter to the skillet and bring to a boil. Reduce for 2 mins.

8. Add shrimp, parsley, pasta, and salt and pepper to taste. Gently mix.

9. Garnish with remaining parsley and serve immediately.

*O*ne of my favorite things to do is to invite women I love over for a "Girls' Night Out." I am blessed to work with an incredible group of women at the *Today Show*. They are among the smartest, hardest-working, most devoted women I have ever known. And they are <u>FUN</u>! Think that's easy at 4am?

Early in the fall of 2013 I invited them for a night of celebration, a world away from the reality of network television. Thank you, Ladies. You give me hope for the future.

The ladies of Today who
make it such a joy to go to
work so early in the morning!

September 2013

SEAFOOD SALAD

MAKES 4 SERVINGS

Ingredients

- 2 lbs large cooked shrimp, sliced in half lengthwise
- 8 oz imitation crab stick (sushi), shredded
- 2 cups celery, coarsly chopped
- 4 oz fresh-squeezed lemon juice (about 2 lemons)
- ½ cup mayonnaise
- 2½ tbsp parsley, finely chopped
- 1 whole lemon, quartered

Directions

1. In a large mixing or salad bowl add shrimp, crab meat, celery, lemon juice, mayonnaise, and 2 tbsp of parsley. Gently mix together incorporating all ingredients.

2. Refrigerate covered for one hour and stir prior to serving. Garnish with remaining parsley and lemon wedges, and enjoy!

NEW WINE IS STORED

IN NEW WINESKINS

SO THAT BOTH ARE PRESERVED.

Matthew 9:17

October

TASTE AND SEE THAT THE LORD IS GOOD,
BLESSED IS THE MAN WHO TAKES REFUGE IN HIM.

Psalm 34:8

October

October 30, 2012, was a terrible and tragic day for many people living in the New York, Connecticut, New Jersey area. The newspapers had been full of foreboding headlines for days before—FRANKENSTORM! And their most dire predictions sadly came true.

Hurricane Sandy arrived with devastating results. Entire neighborhoods were washed away, the lower New York City subway system was flooded, and parts of the New Jersey and New York coastlines were destroyed. People lost their lives, their livelihoods, their pets, their homes, and their treasures.

It was the worst of nature while simultaneously it brought out the best of human nature, as all disasters both man-made and natural inevitably do.

Sitting in our house, built in 1929 on solid rock, some 20 feet above sea level, Frank and I weathered the storm with some of our neighbors. We had been through many storms together in the past but this one, we all knew, was going to be different.

I actually have a sweet memory of all of us huddled together that night, feasting on Joanie's spaghetti, drinking wine, and listening as the fierce wind howled and the tiles on our roof crashed to the ground for hours all around us.

We found solace in the blazing fire and strange comfort we found in each other as the storm raged on.

But early in the morning after a sleepless night, we surveyed the damage and it was clear, even by dawn's early light, that we were going to be cleaning up and rebuilding for weeks and probably months beyond the storm.

Some of our neighbors stayed almost a week. I was so grateful for our generator and thankful that the damage was just to property that can be replaced, and not to people, who can't. A musical that I had spent 13 years writing and re-writing over and over and over again, was scheduled to finally open on November 15th at the Neil Simon Theater on East 52nd Street on Broadway. My show became yet another casualty of the storm. *Scandalous* closed on December 9th and I was broken-hearted in a way I had never experienced before. And yet God was faithful and eventually the whole experience took its rightful place among the great disappointments in my life that although painful, were survivable.

And then winter came.

And winter is an interesting time in nature. Everything goes dormant here. Everything is leafless and lifeless. Or so it seems. It's a time of waiting and trusting. It can be a dark, frustrating time as you freeze and plow and scrape and shiver.

But eventually—finally—spring returns and with it, so does the truth: what you assumed was sleeping is sometimes actually dead.

You find out in spring what you actually lost months before.

I remember sitting on our small patio at the end of our backyard in early March, 2013. The snow was finally cleared and with it, it was clear what had not survived the devastating storm.

250-year-old trees had been downed—we knew that—but more than fifty percent of our foliage also never recovered from Sandy's rage. Now, I was keenly aware of what others had lost and we had lost <u>nothing</u> in comparison. But God used this particular moment in my life to teach me a powerful lesson: He never changes! People do, landscapes do, seasons do, and politics do. But He is the same yesterday, today and forever. (*Hebrews 8:13*)

So as I looked on the damage, despairing, He spoke very gently to my wounded heart. And this is what I heard Him say, "Kathie, I have brought you through many storms much worse than this one. I have been faithful in every trial. I am in the business of bringing beauty from ashes. So, let's make something far more beautiful than it was before."

Immediately I said to Andy, "And, do you think you could get some of your guys here and clear out some of this mess, and maybe we can make this patio a little bigger?"

Andy is one of my favorite people on the planet because he said, as he always says, "It could happen." And then he made it happen. Within hours several of the guys from his landscaping business, Fair-Way, appeared and suddenly we had views we'd never imagined. As they cleared the brush, the debris, and the death of Hurricane Sandy it became obvious that the devastation was actually a spectacular blessing in disguise.

We got to work and beauty emerged. Beauty from ashes. Life from death. Hope. Resurrection. Joy. Abundance. Wow. Wow, God. And thank you.

BECAUSE OF THE LORD'S GREAT LOVE WE ARE NOT CONSUMED,
FOR HIS COMPASSION NEVER FAILS. THEY ARE NEW EVERY MORNING;
GREAT IS YOUR FAITHFULNESS.

Lamentations 3:22-23

Joy Bauer actually makes "healthy" delicious!

*J*oy Bauer is one of the most "contagious" people you will ever meet. She is devoted to helping people find the inner strength to overcome their bad habits and find a brand new healthy and delicious lifestyle.

As the nutrition and health expert at the *Today Show*, she introduces America to new members of the Joy Fit Club--men and women from all over the country who have lost over 100 pounds by changing their nutritional patterns and their exercise routines.

Joy is the perky cheerleader we all need when we're trying to change our lives for the good. She recently introduced her delicious new Nourish Snacks to the market. I was delighted to ask her to also contribute a few of her heart-healthy recipes.

Thank you, Joy, for all you do to encourage people who are hurting and in need of a plan!

Joy's Buffalo Chicken Chili

MAKES 4 SERVINGS

Ingredients

- 6 carrots, peeled, halved lengthwise, and sliced into half-moons
- 6 stalks celery, sliced
- 6 cloves garlic, minced
- 2 pounds chicken, ground (99% lean)
- 2 tbsp chili powder
- 2 tbsp flour, all-purpose
- 4 cups vegetable juice (low-sodium) or tomato juice
- ¼ cup hot sauce, or more to taste (see note)

Optional Toppings:

- sour cream, light or fat-free
- yogurt, nonfat, greek-style
- scallions or green onions
- whipped blue cheese topping, recipe below

Directions

1. Liberally coat a large pot or Dutch oven with oil spray, and preheat over medium-high heat. Add carrots and celery and sauté, stirring occasionally, until tender, about 10 minutes. Add water, a tablespoon at a time, as necessary to prevent scorching.

2. Add garlic and sauté for 1 minute. Add the ground chicken, reapplying oil spray if necessary. Sauté, stirring continuously and breaking chicken into small pieces, for 5 minutes or until cooked through. As the chicken cooks, continue scraping the bottom of pan with a wooden spoon to dislodge any large bits.

3. Sprinkle in chili powder and flour, and stir quickly to distribute them evenly. Immediately add vegetable juice and hot sauce, and bring to a boil. Reduce the heat to low and simmer, partially covered, stirring occasionally, for about 20 minutes.

4. Ladle the chili into serving bowls and serve with desired toppings.

NOTE: *The amount of hot sauce you use will depend on the brand you select as well as your own personal tolerance for spicy foods. Start with ¼ cup hot sauce to start with, then tasting the chili and adding more if you find it too mild.*

Whipped Blue Cheese Topping:

In a small bowl mash together ¼ cup blue cheese crumbles (at room temperature) and ¼ cup sour cream (light/nonfat) or greek yogurt (nonfat, plain). Dollop on top of chili before serving.

Joy's Autumn Cocktails: Berkshire Iced Tea

makes 1 serving

Ingredients

- 1 lemon-ginger tea bag
- 8 oz boiling water
- 2 oz grapefruit juice
- chopped mint
- ½ oz vodka (optional)
- ½ oz rum (optional)

MINT ICE CUBES:

- grapefruit juice or water
- chopped mint

Directions

1. Freeze mint ice cubes in advance by adding chopped mint to an ice cube tray filled with grapefruit juice or filtered water.

2. Steep lemon-ginger tea bag in 8 ounces of boiling water. Allow to cool in refrigerator.

3. Once cooled, remove tea bag and pour into a large glass. Add 2 ounces of grapefruit juice and a couple leaves of chopped mint.

4. For adult spin, add optional ½ ounce vodka and ½ ounce rum.

5. Stir, add lots of ice and enjoy!

30 calories without alcohol; 80 calories with alcohol

Andy making his chef's debut on Today,
October 2013.

Andy's Chorizo Fondue
in a pumpkin bowl

Ingredients

- 1 - 2-3 lb sugar pumpkin (seasonal)
- 8 oz dried chorizo, 4-6 oz diced
- fresh roasted new mexico green chili (seasonal); Can substitute fresh roasted poblanos (with skins and seeds removed) or canned green chili.
- 2 pinches ground cumin
- 1 pinch cayenne pepper

- 4 tbsp all-purpose flour
- 1 ½ cups chicken broth
- 2 cups shredded mozzarella cheese or Oaxaca mexican cheese
- 1 cup shredded mexican cheese (mix of monterrey jack, cheddar, queso quesadilla, asadero cheese)

Directions

1. Preheat oven to 375 degrees. Remove top of pumpkin near stem, approximately 5-6" diameter of pumpkin, and remove seeds and pulp. Clear it out well as this your fondue bowl. Careful not to thin out walls and base too much in order to maintain structure.

2. In a medium-sized stock pot, heat chorizo over medium-high heat until fat begins to melt, about 3-5 minutes, stirring frequently. Add diced green chili, cayenne pepper, and cumin and cook for 2 minutes, until incorporated. Add flour and cook, stirring until well blended, about 2 minutes.

3. Add chicken broth and bring to a gentle boil. Reduce heat to medium and begin adding cheeses. Heat, stirring occasionally for 2-3 minutes or until all cheese has melted to a creamy consistency. Remove from heat.

4. Place pumpkin in a small, oven-safe baking dish. Using a ladle, fill pumpkin with melted cheese until almost full (1 inch from the top).

5. Add approximately 1 inch of hot water to baking dish surrounding pumpkin. Loosely cover pumpkin with foil and bake until tender, about 1 hour. Remove foil and bake for additional 15-20 minutes.

6. Remove from oven and let stand for 5-10 minutes. Transfer to separate platter, being careful to support bottom of pumpkin with sturdy spatula.

7. Serve immediately with sturdy tortilla chips! Enjoy!

The first autumn in our new home, 1994.

*W*e live outdoors as much as possible until the boats disappear and the flower pots and window boxes are stored for the winter in late October. I admit I go into a bit of a funk when the first frost comes and I prepare for the inevitable bleakness that's right around the corner. But then we start making those roaring fires and settle in for a long winter's nap and start dreaming of crocuses again as the autumn leaves fall.

THE LORD MAKE HIS FACE TO SHINE UPON YOU
AND BE GRACIOUS TO YOU. THE LORD LIFT UP
HIS COUNTENANCE UPON YOU AND GIVE YOU PEACE.

Numbers 6: 25-26

November

THE LORD IS MY STRENGTH AND SHIELD.
I TRUST HIM WITH ALL MY HEART.
HE HELPS ME AND MY HEART IS FILLED WITH JOY.
I BURST OUT IN SONGS OF THANKSGIVING.

Psalm 28:7

November

I adore Thanksgiving because since the very first celebration in Plymouth, Massachusetts, in 1621, it has continued to be about one thing: GRATITUDE.

Gratefulness for God's provision, for His blessing, and for His abundance in our every day lives.

I think we should celebrate that every day of the year, because when we lose sight of the Giver of all good gifts, we have lost sight of everything that really matters.

I don't cook much in our home throughout the year but I do try to make up for it on Thanksgiving. We start several days before the feast and I love the whole process. If I'm not covered in flour and cinnamon and sage and gravy by the time we sit down to give thanks to God Almighty, I have slacked off and I am not worthy of praise! I'm so grateful for the joy of family and friends and food and fellowship.

Is there anything sweeter?

GIVE THANKS TO THE LORD FOR HE IS GOOD;
HIS LOVE ENDURES FOREVER.

Psalm 107:1

Joanie's Sage & Sausage Thanksgiving Stuffing

Makes enough to stuff a 20 lb turkey

Ingredients

- ½ cup butter (1 stick)
- 8 celery ribs, chopped
- 1 large onion, peeled and chopped
- 2 lbs pork sausage, casing removed
- 2 packages (16 oz each) herb seasoned stuffing
- 1-2 tbsp ground sage
- salt and pepper to taste

Directions

1. In a large saucepan, heat the butter over medium-high heat. Add the celery and onion for 10-15 minutes, or until vegetables are softened.

2. In a large skillet, cook sausage over medium-high heat until cooked through. Drain the fat from the meat and discard.

3. In a large bowl, combine the vegetable mixture, cooked sausage, and bread croutons. Add a little water to moisten the stuffing slightly. Season with sage, salt, and pepper.

4. Stuff turkey cavity and cook as directed.

5. Bake any leftover stuffing in a buttered baking dish.

THE LORD IS RIGHTEOUS IN ALL HIS WAYS

AND LOVING TOWARD ALL HE HAS MADE.

THE LORD IS NEAR TO ALL WHO CALL ON HIM,

TO ALL WHO CALL ON HIM IN TRUTH.

Psalm 145:17-18

Learning how to make Grandma Joanie's sensational stuffing.

Thanksgiving, 1997

Michie's Sweet Potato Soufflé

makes 8-10 servings

Ingredients

- 3 lbs sweet potatoes or yams, peeled and cut into cubes
- 2 large eggs
- ¾ cup firmly packed brown sugar, divided
- ½ cup (1 stick) butter, melted and divided
- 1 tsp salt
- 1 tsp ground cinnamon
- up to ½ cup orange juice
- 1 cup pecan halves

Directions

1. Preheat oven to 375 degrees.

2. In a large saucepan over high heat, add potatoes and enough water to cover them, and bring to a boil. Reduce the heat, cover, and simmer for 15-20 minutes, or until the potatoes are soft. Drain.

3. In a large bowl, beat the potatoes with an electric mixer until they are smooth. Beat in the eggs, ¼ cup of brown sugar, ¼ cup of butter, salt, and cinnamon. Starting with ¼ cup, beat in just enough orange juice to make the mixture moist and fluffy.

4. Scrape the sweet potato mixture into a 2-3 quart soufflé dish and smooth the surface into an even layer. Arrange the pecan halves over the top. Sprinkle the remaining ½ cup of brown sugar over the pecans. Drizzle the top with the remaining ¼ cup of melted butter.

5. Bake for 25 -30 minutes, or until the top is bubbly all over.

Shannie's Pumpkin Trifle

MAKES 4 SERVINGS

Ingredients

- 2 - 14 oz packages pumpkin bread mix (we use Pillsbury Quick Bread)
- 1 - 5.1 oz instant vanilla pudding mix
- 1 - 30 oz can pumpkin
- ½ cup brown sugar
- ⅓ tsp ground cinnamon
- 1 - 12 oz frozen whipped topping
- ½ cup gingersnaps

Directions

1. Bake the pumpkin bread according to package instructions and cool completely.

2. Meanwhile, prepare pudding and set aside. If using cook-and-serve pudding mix, allow to cool completely.

3. Stir pumpkin, sugar, and cinnamon into pudding.

4. Crumble 1 batch of bread into bottom of trifle bowl. Pour half of pudding mixture over crumbled pumpkin bread, then add a layer of whipped topping. Repeat with remaining pumpkin bread, pudding, and whipped topping. Sprinkle top with crushed gingersnaps.

5. Refrigerate overnight.

NOTE: *It's important to have a trifle bowl with a stand or some kind of bowl that shows the layers of the trifle.*

I was stunned this past November, when just as I thought that Mother Nature had gone to hibernate for the winter, a rose bush bloomed in all of its glory. It didn't last long, but long enough to remind me that God is full of surprises.

FORGET THE FORMER THINGS,
DO NOT DWELL ON THE PAST.
SEE, I AM DOING A NEW THING.
NOW IT SPRINGS UP;
DO YOU NOT PERCEIVE IT?
I AM MAKING A WAY IN THE DESERT
AND STREAMS IN THE WASTELAND.

Isaiah 43:18-19

IN YOUR LOVE AND MERCY YOU REDEEM ME.

YOU LIFT ME UP AND CARRY ME

AS YOU HAVE DONE FOR YOUR CHILDREN

THROUGH ALL OF THE DAYS OF OLD.

Isaiah 43:3

ENTER HIS GATES
WITH THANKSGIVING AND
HIS COURTS WITH PRAISE;
GIVE THANKS TO HIM
AND PRAISE HIS NAME.

Psalm 100:4

Thanksgiving with Frank, Joanie, my brother Dave, his wife Sandy,
Me, Cody, my niece Shannie, her husband Mark, my sister Michie, and
her husband Craig. Cassidy was in California.

*N*ovember 13, 2002. A blustery, grey, nasty day. And a truly painful day because I was about to leave our house to travel to Delaware to bring my Daddy home from the hospital to die. Hospice=Hopeless. The doctors had done all they could do for him. And we were about to start doing what only his loved ones could do: Help him pass gently from this life to the next. To Jesus.

I had a few moments before the car arrived to take me to the airport. I stepped out onto the patio off our sunroom just to breathe some much needed air. Air=Life. And I needed a reason to keep on living. My Daddy was the finest person I have ever been privileged to know and everyone who ever knew him feels the same way. The weight of the loss of him was searing my soul and life without him seemed completely impossible. So there on the patio, under the 200-year-old tree where I had shared so much life with him, I prayed a prayer for help. I prayed to Abba, my Father God, to help me through the loss of Eppie, my beloved earthly Daddy.

"Lord," I cried into the wind, "I can't even imagine a life without him. Please give me a sign that I'll never really lose my Daddy. That he'll always be with me. Or else, take me, too, Lord, because it's just too hard to bear."

Immediately, I looked up into the heavens; but there-high on a branch on the barren tree, was the last leaf before winter claimed it. There it was, hanging on for dear life, just like my Daddy was.

I gasped at the sight of it. I rejoiced at the wonder of it. And thanking God with tears streaming down my grief-filled face, I walked back into the sunroom and wrote these words:

HE IS WITH YOU

Lyrics by Kathie Lee Gifford

Old man winter is creeping up the hill

I can hear his icy fingers tapping on the window sill

I can see his frosty footsteps as he whistles thru the weeds

And the little squirrel hurries to gather what he needs.

Old mother nature is dressing in her cloak

As the last leaf dances on the branches of the oak

It's time to draw the curtains as the fall draws to a close

And listen to the secret only mother nature knows.

He is with you

All who've come before and gone, go on here with you

As a new dawn breaks, new life awakes within you

As sure as every flower reaches to the sun

He is with you

Unseen by human eyes He breathes the air

And whispers up a prayer

That you will hear his sighs

And you will realize

He's there

In the glowing embers, in the frozen riverbed

Mother Nature dreams her summer dreams

as snow falls overhead

The rose is only sleeping, and soon, before too long

The daffodil will waken to the sparrow's tender song

He is with you

All who've come before and gone go on here with you

Though they seem to disappear

They're here, still with you

Sure as every mountain reaches to the sky

He is with you

He is reaching out his arms to hold you near

Year after lonely year

And he will never leave

As long as you believe he's here

No, you'll never have to grieve

As long as you believe

He's here

The dogwood only slumbers, and soon she too shall wake

And the swan will swim with her children again

on the silent, silvery lake.

A few years later my good friend and collaborator, David Pomeranz, wrote a gorgeous melody to these lyrics and we incorporated it into our musical, *Under The Bridge*, which premiered Off Broadway in 2003. I think everyone who has ever lost anyone who is precious to them can relate and even to this day, every time I walk under my Daddy's tree, I cry out in praise and gratitude for the gift of him. The wondrous gift of my daddy.

My hand in my daddy's hand, just before we gave him up to God.

THE SEEDS OF GOOD DEEDS BECOME A TREE OF LIFE.

Proverbs 11:30

December

LOOK! THE VIRGIN WILL CONCEIVE A CHILD!
SHE WILL GIVE BIRTH TO A SON
AND THEY WILL CALL HIM IMMANUEL,
WHICH MEANS GOD IS WITH US.

Matthew 1:23

December

For many, Christmas morning conjures up images of sugar and spice and cinnamon and surprises under the Christmas tree. But in our home we have always tried to make Christmas morning about the special, extraordinary miracle of Christ's birth. Years ago a wise friend told me that if I wanted to keep Christmas truly about Christmas for my family I should limit my children's gifts to the three presents baby Jesus received from the Magi who came to visit Him. This simple tradition transformed our holiday celebration! It centered the day on the true meaning and as a result, it transformed our children's lives forever. I doubt they remember many of the gifts they received but they do remember Who came into the world to redeem it. They learned that Christmas is not about stuff. It's about Him. And hope for all of mankind.

FOR IT IS BY GRACE THAT YOU
HAVE BEEN SAVED, THROUGH FAITH —
AND THIS NOT FROM YOURSELVES,
IT IS THE GIFT OF GOD.

Ephesians 2:8

Joanie always made a Swedish pastry on Christmas morning when we were growing up. It's called "Kringa" but of course Joanie, in her special style, got it wrong and called it "Klinga." Whatever. We all called it delicious! And we still do.

The beautiful painting, *A Joyful Noise Unto The Lord*, is by my favorite new artist and new friend, Anne H. Neilson, and was my favorite gift this past Christmas. My precious "steadfast friends", Emilie and Craig Wierda, surprised me with it. Their friendship is yet another priceless gift from the Lord.

Joanie's Kringa

makes 20 servings

Crust Ingredients

- 1 cup all-purpose flour
- ½ cup (1 stick) unsalted chilled butter,
  cut into ½ inch cubes
- 2 tbsp ice water, divided

Puff Ingredients

- 1 cup water
- ½ cup (1 stick) unsalted butter
- 4 cups confectioners sugar
- 2 tbsp milk, divided
- 1 tsp vanilla or almond extract

Buttercream Ingredients

- 8 tbsp (1 stick) butter, softened
- 3-4 cups 10x confectioners sugar
- 3-4 tbsp milk
- 1 tsp vanilla or almond extract.

Directions

To make crust:

1. Place flour and butter in large bowl. Using pastry blender, or 2 knives used scissor-fashion, work butter into flour until pieces are no larger than peas.

2. Sprinkle 1 tbsp of ice water over flour mixture and stir with fork until it begins to hold together. Press dough into ball. (If dough remains dry and crumbly, sprinkle 1 tbsp of water over dough and stir until it holds together.) Divide dough in half and wrap pieces in plastic. Refrigerate for about 1 hour, or until firm.

3. Lightly dust one piece of chilled dough with flour and pat into rectangle. Place between two sheets of waxed paper and roll into a strip that measures about 13" x 4". Peel off top sheet of waxed paper and invert dough onto 15½" x 10½" jelly-roll pan, leaving room for second piece of dough. Peel off second sheet of waxed paper. (If paper is difficult to remove, chill the dough on the jellyroll pan until the dough is firm.) Trim dough so edges are straight. Repeat with second piece of dough. Refrigerate while you make puff.

To make puff:

4. Preheat oven to 375 degrees. In medium saucepan, warm water and butter over medium heat until butter is melted. Increase heat to medium-high and bring to boil. Remove pan from heat. Add flour and stir vigorously until batter smooth. Transfer to large bowl. One at a time, add eggs, beating well after each addition. Stir in vanilla or almond extract.

5. Remove dough from refrigerator. Spread half of puff mixture in an even layer over each strip. Bake 35-40 minutes, or until golden brown and puff layer is dry and firm. Cool pan completely on wire rack.

To make buttercream:

6. In large bowl, beat butter until smooth. Gradually add confectioners sugar, beating on medium-high until smooth. Add enough milk to make a creamy, spreadable consistency. Beat in vanilla or almond extract. Divide in half and spread evenly over each cooled pastry. Slice each diagonally into 10 slices.

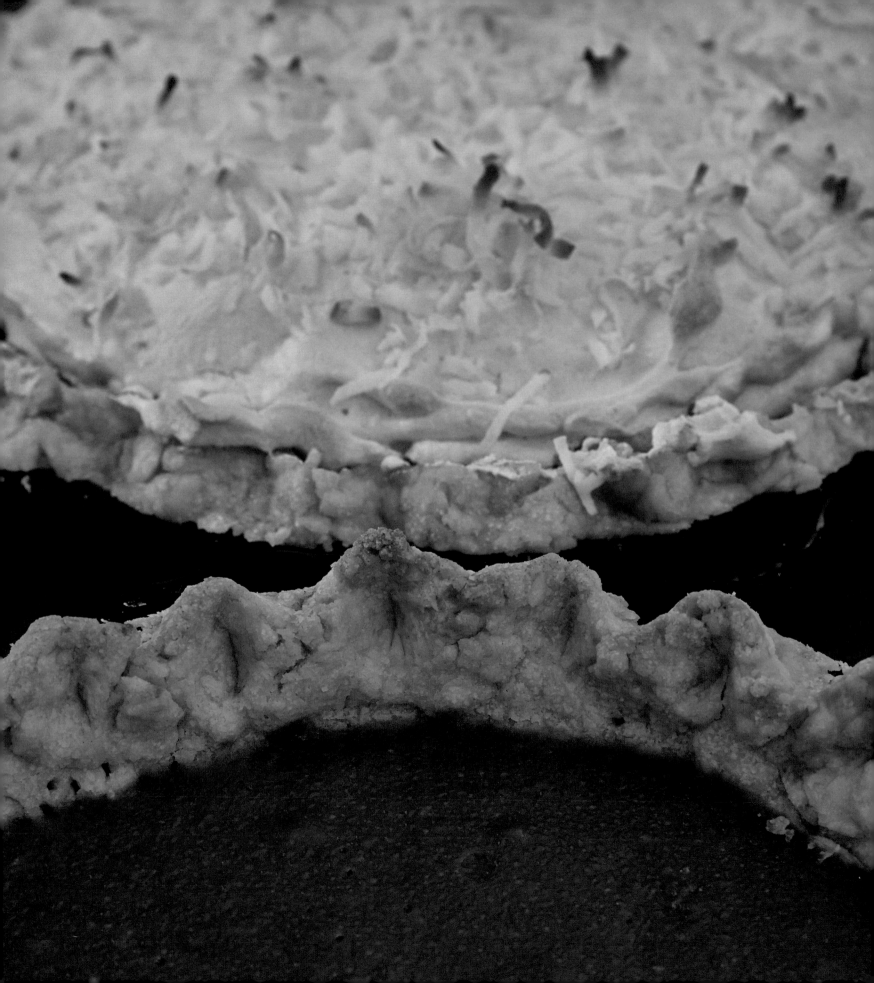

Sandy's Custard Pies

Custard Ingredients

- ¾ cup sugar
- 4 tbsp flour
- 3 eggs
- ¼ cup milk
- 1 can Carnation evaporated milk
- ½ cup water
- 1 tbsp butter
- ½ tsp vanilla
- pre-baked pie crust

Meringue Ingredients

- 1 tbsp. cornstarch
- 2 tbsp. cold water
- ½ cup boiling water
- 3 egg whites, at room temperature
- 6 tbsp sugar
- 1 tsp vanilla
- dash of salt

Directions

1. In a bowl, thoroughly mix sugar, flour, eggs and milk, and set aside.

2. In the top of a double boiler combine evaporated milk and water. Whisk in sugar-flour mixture until smooth. Cook over simmering water, whisking constantly, until mixture thickens to a pudding-like consistency. Remove from heat and whisk in butter and vanilla.

3. Add ingredients for one of the following flavor variations:

For Chocolate Custard Pie: Add some good-quality milk chocolate to the hot mixture and stir until it melts completely. (I use Cadbury Milk Chocolate; Do not using baking chocolate.) Pour into baked pie shell. After pie cools, top with whipped cream and refrigerate.

For Banana Cream Pie: Slice bananas and put them into the bottom of a cooled baked pie crust. Pour prepared custard on top of bananas. After pie cools, top with whipped cream and refrigerate.

For Coconut Custard Pie: Add some sweetened coconut to the custard mixture before you pour it into the baked pie shell. Top with *Never Fail Meringue* (recipe below) and bake as directed.

Never Fail Merigue:

1. In a saucepan, combine cornstarch and cold water. Add ½ cup boiling water and stir mixture until thickened and clear. Set aside until cooled to lukewarm or room temperature. *(Can make ahead or refrigerate if in hurry.)*

2. While waiting for it to cool: Mix egg whites, on high, until foamy. Gradually add sugar and beat until thickened. Turn mixer to low and add vanilla and salt.

3. With mixer on high, gradually beat in cool cornstarch mixture. Spread on pie, sprinkle top with coconut, and bake at 350 degrees for 10 minutes or until light brown. Refrigerate when cool.

January

THE EARTH IS THE LORD'S, AND EVERYTHING IN IT.
BLESSED BE THE NAME OF THE LORD.

Psalm 24:1

COME TO ME, ALL YOU WHO LABOR

AND ARE HEAVY-LADEN

AND I WILL GIVE YOU REST

Matthew 11:28

January

I have vague memories of a time when I adored winter, but I must admit, it's so long ago that I can hardly remember! When I was a little girl growing up in Maryland it seemed like the winters were like the ones described in the C.S. Lewis classic, *Chronicles of Narnia*, but it must be because I was so small in stature that the snow drifts seemed like mountains and the hot chocolate that greeted my brother and sister and me when we finally came inside was right out of *Willie Wonka & The Chocolate Factory!* One winter I swear we built an igloo that lasted two months. Such is the fog of childhood memories and I wouldn't want to ever lose them.

Then, for a few years when our kids were little, we owned a beautiful home in Colorado and experienced magical Rocky Mountain High Christmases complete with horse drawn sleighs and real foot long icicles. I felt like we lived in a dream.

But now I'm 60 and I finally admit the truth. I find it hard to like anything about winter at all except that I do love a roaring good fire with my fragrant candles flickering on the mantle. *BUT NOT FOR 4 MONTHS IN A ROW!*

So we escape whenever we get a chance for a few days of sunshine and bougainvilleas. But when we can't get away I look at the indoor window boxes that I installed out of desperation when I was diagnosed with S.A.D.—Seasonal Affected Disorder. I was so happy to discover that I wasn't "crazy"—there was indeed a chemical reason that I was battling depression during the grey, dreary, drizzly winter months. And I wasn't alone! Millions of others do, too! Who needs more guilt, right? It's chemical, right? I'm not crazy, right? Right? Ok, A little. But I don't trust anyone who isn't a little crazy.

COMMIT YOUR WAY TO THE LORD,

TRUST ALSO IN HIM, AND HE WILL DO IT.

Psalm 37:5

"Swannie", our favorite swan. Winter doesn't bother her a bit.

When my beautiful mother, Joan Nancy Cuttell, was growing up the boys used to call her "Cuddles." It's easy to still see why. "Joanie," as she is known to all now is one of the sunniest, happiest, people you will ever meet. It could be the coldest day on the planet, and she would still exude warmth.

She couldn't boil water when she married my daddy at age 19. She has become an extraordinary cook over the years and many of the recipes in this collection are hers—a million memories of special times with the thing that she has always cherished the most—her family—because she had lost most of her family by the time she was 15.

We celebrated Joanie on January 20th, her 84th birthday, with her special spaghetti.

Mangia, Mommy! We love you.

Joanie's Spaghetti

Ingredients

- 2 lbs ground beef
- 4 large cans Hunt's tomato sauce
- 1 large can Hunt's tomato paste
- 2 tbsp olive oil
- ¾ cup dried parsley flakes
- ¼ tsp oregano

- 1 tbsp garlic powder or chilled minced garlic (we use minced)
- 1 large onion, diced
- Salt and pepper to taste

Directions

1. In a large pot or dutch oven, brown the ground beef over medium-high heat until no pink remains. Break up clumps of meat as they form.

2. Stir in remaining ingredients and bring to a boil. Lower to a simmer and cook for 1-2 hours, stirring often.

MAY THE LORD RICHLY BLESS
YOU AND YOUR CHILDREN.
MAY YOU BE BLESSED BY THE LORD
WHO MADE HEAVEN AND EARTH.

Psalm 115:14,15

Mom, Michie, and Me

*O*n the day of our January photo session for *Good Gifts* I woke up to huge flakes of snow falling from a grey sky. No snow had been in the forecast but we were thrilled. It created the perfect atmosphere for us to shoot our recipes for stuffed game hens with winter vegetables and mashed potatoes.

This pub room is part of an addition we did in 2000 when I left *"Live with Regis & Kathie Lee"* and it's one of my favorite rooms in the winter time. It's perfect for a lunch or dinner for six and we always tend to linger long after because it's just hard to leave the peace and serenity of it.

It's also one of my favorite places to write my books, or screenplays, music or *Everyone Has A Story* lyrics because it's the farthest away from the kitchen where all the action is in everybody's house.

It's a gift.

Oven-Roasted Stuffed Cornish Game Hens

MAKES 6 SERVINGS

Ingredients

- 6 equally-sized cornish game hens
- 2 tbsp extra virgin olive oil
- 1 tbsp Lawry's Seasoned Salt
- 1 tbsp dried parsley flakes
- 1 tbsp poultry seasoning
- ½ tbsp fresh ground pepper
- stuffing mix (see recipe page 67)

Directions

1. Pre-heat oven to 375°.

2. Rinse and dry hens. Rub thouroughly with olive oil, including inside cavity.

3. Mix seasoned salt, pepper, parsley flakes, and poultry seasoning, and sprinkle generously over entire hen and inside body cavity.

4. Loosely stuff cavity with your favorite stuffing mixture, or try *Joanie's Sausage and Sage Stuffing*, page 67.

5. Place hens breast-side up on large baking sheet with rack, leaving space between hens. Use two pans if necessary.

6. Roast for approximately 1 hour, until internal temperature reaches 165° or until juices run clear when poked near leg and thigh.

7. Remove from oven and let rest for about 10 minutes, covered loosely in foil.

Bianca's Lemon Bars

Crust Ingredients

- 2 cups, loosely filled, unbleached all-purpose flour
- 1 cup, loosely filled, confectioners sugar, plus more to garnish
- ¾ tsp salt
- grated zest of 1 lemon
- 12 tbsp (1½ sticks) unsalted butter, cut into ½" pcs.

Filling Ingredients

- 9 large egg yolks, plus 3 large eggs
- 1¾ cups granulated sugar
- 7 plump lemons, zested and juiced (zest of 1 lemon used in crust)
- Pinch of salt
- 8 tbsps unsalted butter, cut into ½"pieces

Directions

1. Spray 9x13" metal baking pan with non-stick cooking spray. Line pan with 13"-wide piece of foil, long enough to extend 1" over each long top edge of pan. Spray lightly with cooking spray. Fit second sheet of foil, 9" wide, in pan in the same manner, perpendicular to first sheet. Spray once more with non-stick cooking spray.

2. Place flour, confectioners sugar, salt and lemon zest in food processor and process briefly. Add butter and process until the mixture resembles coarse meal, but is not yet forming a ball. Transfer mixture to prepared pan and press into an even layer over bottom of pan, not up the sides. Refrigerate about ½ hour.

3. Preheat oven to 350 degrees and place rack in center. Assemble ingredients for filling while oven heats. Bake crust until light golden brown, about 20 minutes. Reduce temperature to 300 degrees. (Make filling while crust bakes so that it's ready while the crust is still hot.)

4. In non-reactive saucepan, whisk together egg yolks and whole eggs until combined. Whisk in granulated sugar, 1 cup lemon juice*, zest and salt, until well blended. Place pan over medium-low heat and cook, stirring constantly with rubber spatula, until mixture thickens. Stop occasionally to whisk well. Once mixture has thickened slightly, remove from heat.

5. Place butter pieces into a clean glass bowl. Pour the hot filling through stainless steel mesh strainer into the bowl, pressing filling through the strainer. Whisk the butter and filling until smooth, then pour onto warm crust. Return to oven and bake until filling jiggles only slightly when shaken, 16-20 minutes. Cool completely on wire rack. If desired, refrigerate lemon bars 1-2 hours, or overnight, before cutting. Remove bars from pan using overhanging foil and transfer to cutting board. Cut into squares or bars. Sift confectioners sugar over bars just before serving.

*Any remaining lemon juice can be frozen for future use.

FROM THE DEW OF HEAVEN AND

THE RICHNESS OF THE EARTH,

MAY GOD ALWAYS GIVE YOU

ABUNDANT HARVESTS OF GRAIN

AND BOUNTIFUL NEW WINE.

Genesis 27:28

I AM THE VINE,
YOU ARE THE BRANCHES.
HE WHO ABIDES IN ME,
AND I IN HIM, BEARS MUCH FRUIT;
FOR WITHOUT ME,
YOU CAN DO NOTHING.

John 15:5

February

SPENDOR AND MAJESTY ARE BEFORE HIM.
STRENGTH AND GLORY ARE IN HIS SANCTUARY.

Psalm 96:6

DO NOT GRIEVE, FOR THE JOY OF
THE LORD IS YOUR STRENGTH!

Nehemiah 8:10

February

Very early in our marriage our Super Bowl parties became the hottest ticket in town. It seems everybody wanted to watch the big game with Frank. So a Super Bowl party became almost a prerequisite of our continuing friendships. We go all out and are never sorry we did. Frank always insists on playing my rendition of the National Anthem in 1995 before he lets anyone eat and every year I beg him not to, to no avail.

Oh well. It's once a year.

Elvia's Guacamole

Ingredients

- 6 large ripe avocados
- 4 cups italian tomatoes, diced (cut into quarters and remove seeds prior to chopping)
- 1 cup white onion, finely diced
- 4 tbsp fresh jalapeño, finely diced, seeds and veins removed (about 2 large jalapeños)

- 1 cup cilantro, coarsely diced
- salt and pepper to taste
- 1 bag tortilla chips, scoop-shaped or restaurant-style

- reserve a few sprigs of cilantro and small handful of tomato for garnish

Directions

1. Cut avocados in half. Remove pit (set aside) and skin. Cut into ¼" - ½" cubes.

2. In a large bowl combine avocado, tomatoes, onion, jalapeño, and cilantro. Mix thoroughly. Add salt and pepper to taste. Garnish with sprigs of cilantro and diced tomato.

3. Serve immediately with tortilla chips.

BLESSED ARE THOSE WHO HAVE LEARNED TO ACCLAIM YOU,

WHO WALK IN THE LIGHT OF YOUR PRESENCE, O LORD.

THEY REJOICE IN YOUR NAME ALL DAY LONG;

THEY EXALT IN YOUR RIGHTEOUSNESS.

Psalm 89:15-16

Super Bowl Chili

MAKES 10 SERVINGS

Ingredients

- 2 tbsp olive oil
- 1 white onion, diced (about 1 cup)
- 1 large red bell pepper, diced (about 1 cup)
- 2 large carrots, diced (about 1 cup)
- 2 tsp ground cumin
- 1 lb lean ground beef (90% lean)
- 1 can each, drained and rinsed:
    Pinto, Kidney, and Black Beans
- 1 large can (28 oz) crushed tomatoes
- 2 tbsp red chili powder

- 1 small can La Costeña Chipotle Pepper in Adobo Sauce, of which you will use:
    - 3 tsp adobo sauce
    - 1 whole chipotle pepper, seeded and minced (or more if desired)
- ½ tsp dried oregano
- 2 cups water
- Lawry's Seasoned Salt
- fresh cracked pepper to taste

Directions

1. In a large pot or dutch oven, warm oil over medium heat, careful not to burn. Add red bell peppers, onion, and carrots, and sauté, stirring occasionally until carrots are soft, approximately 7-10 minutes.

2. Add cumin and incorporate with vegetables.

3. Increase heat to medium-high and add ground beef. Stir frequently, using a wooden spoon to break up meat, until beef is no longer pink.

4. Add tomatoes, chili powder, chipotle pepper, adobo sauce, oregano, water, a dash or two of Lowry's Season Salt, and fresh cracked pepper.

5. Reduce heat to medium, bringing to constant simmer.

6. Partially cover and cook for 30 minutes, stirring occasionally.

7. Add beans and partially cover, cooking for an additional 20 minutes.

8. Remove from heat; let stand for 10 minutes.

9. Add additional Lowry's Season Salt and fresh cracked pepper to taste.

WHOM HAVE I IN HEAVEN BUT YOU?

I DESIRE YOU MORE THAN ANYTHING ON EARTH.

MY HEALTH MAY FAIL AND MY SPIRIT MAY GROW WEAK,

BUT GOD REMAINS THE STRENGTH OF MY HEART.

HE IS MINE FOREVER.

Psalm 73:25-26

"Eppie's Tree", waiting patiently for spring.

Chicken Wings

Ingredients

- 3 lb chicken wings, tips removed, wing and drum separated
- 1 cup hot pepper sauce (preferably Frank's Red Hot Sauce)
- ½ tsp worcestershire sauce
- 1½ tbsp white vinegar
- ½ cup unsalted butter
- ½ tsp chili powder
- ¼ tsp garlic power
- salt to taste

Directions

1. In a saucepan, combine hot sauce, vinegar, worcestershire, chili powder, garlic powder and salt, and stir with a whisk. Place over medium heat and add butter, stirring frequently until butter melts. Once sauce begins to bubble remove from heat and set aside.

2. Preheat oven to 450 degrees.

3. Place wings in a large bowl and drizzle with a little olive oil and salt, toss to coat. Lay wings onto a wire rack set over a baking sheet. Wings can touch slightly but should not be overlapping.

4. Wash and dry the bowl and transfer the wing sauce to it. Set aside until needed.

5. Bake the wings in the oven for 15-20 minutes, until golden and crispy on the top. Turn wings over and return to oven for another 10-15 minutes, until cooked through.

6. Transfer the hot wings to the bowl of sauce, tossing well to coat evenly.

7. Serve immediately and enjoy!

THIS IS THE DAY THAT THE LORD HAS MADE.

LET US REJOICE AND BE GLAD IN IT!

Psalm 118:24

THEREFORE DO NOT WORRY ABOUT TOMORROW,

FOR TOMORROW WILL WORRY ABOUT ITSELF.

Matthew 6:34

March

THERE IS A TIME FOR EVERYTHING, AND
A SEASON FOR EVERY ACTIVITY UNDER HEAVEN.

Ecclesiastes 3:1

Daddy and Cody in 1990, in his beloved Rehoboth Beach

March

I have bittersweet memories of March, the windiest month of the year. My beloved Daddy was born on March 19th and my son, Cody, was born on March 22nd. And March is when we get crocuses, forsythia and daffodils. So the way I see it, there are 5 reasons to appreciate March. I'm open to suggestions if you can think of any more.

Wait — I thought of a good one! St. Patrick's Day!

GIVE FREELY AND BECOME MORE WEALTHY;
BE STINGY, AND LOSE EVERYTHING.
THE GENEROUS WILL PROSPER,
THOSE WHO REFRESH OTHERS
WILL THEMSELVES BE REFRESHED.

Proverbs 11:24-25

HE HAS TAKEN ME TO THE
BANQUET HALL AND HIS
BANNER OVER ME IS LOVE.

Song of Songs 2:4

On the day Cody was born, March 22, 1990, God gave our famiy yet another precious gift. Christine Maria Gardner had been working part time for me and Frank for a couple years house-sitting and dog-sitting. But she moved in with us on the day of Cody's birth and became Cody's full-time nanny. The three of us went back to *Live with Regis and Kathie Lee* five weeks later, and Christine became one of Cassidy's godmothers when she was born three and a half years after that.

She now heads my production company and goes in to *Today* with me every day. None of the Giffords could survive without her in our lives and we thank God for her every day. I tease Frank, "Honey, I love you and if you ever left me I'd miss you very much, but if Christine ever left me, I'd kill myself!" He always laughs and says, "Me too!"

Christine's family has also become like family to us, and her mother, Jean, has contributed several of her delicious recipes that are saturated with memories for our kids. Thank you, Grandma Gardner, for loving my children and feeding them all of these years. And thank you, Christine, for simply everything.

Grandma Gardner's
Irish Soda Bread

Ingredients

- 2 cups flour
- 1½ tsp baking powder
- 1 tsp salt
- ¾ tsp baking soda
- 3 tbsp sugar

- 1½ tsp caraway seeds
- 3 tbsp butter
- 1 cup buttermilk
- ⅔ cup raisins

Directions

1. Preheat oven to 350 degrees.

2. Mix together flour, baking powder, salt, baking soda, sugar, and caraway seeds.

3. Cut in 3 tbsp butter, continuing to cut the pieces smaller after added to mixture.

4. Make a well in center of mixture. Add buttermilk and raisins, and stir ingredients together.

5. Fold out onto floured surface. Knead a few turns. Form dough into round and place in greased 9" round pan. Cut crossways through top of dough, roughly two-thirds deep.

6. Bake for 30 minutes or until golden brown. Test with toothpick to make sure it is cooked through.

"Tis a lovely thing for sure!"

(CHOOSE LIFE) THAT YOU MAY LOVE
THE LORD YOUR GOD, LISTEN TO HIS
VOICE, AND HOLD FAST TO HIM.
FOR THE LORD IS YOUR LIFE...

Deuteronomy 30:20

Bianca's Fresh Asparagus Soup
with diced beets

makes 4 servings

Ingredients

- 2 tbsp butter
- ¾ cup fresh white onion, chopped
- 1½ lb fresh asparagus, ends removed and cut into 1" pieces
- 4 cups (32 oz) chicken broth
- 1 tsp fresh-squeezed lemon juice
- 4 toasted croutons (½" thick slices cut from 2-3" baguette)
- 1 cup diced beets, cooked and peeled
- salt and pepper to taste

Directions

1. In a large saucepan, melt butter over medium heat. Add onion and a pinch of salt and pepper, and sauté for 2-3 minutes, stirring frequently. Add asparagus and sauté for additional 2 minutes.

2. Add chicken broth and bring to a boil. Reduce heat, cover, and simmer for 12-15 minutes, stirring frequently. Remove from heat and set aside.

3. In a blender or food processor, add mixture and puree to a smooth consistency. Return to saucepan over low heat.

4. Add lemon juice and salt and pepper to taste. Add crouton to center of serving bowl, then add soup until covered. Add ¼ cup diced beets to the top of crouton for garnish, and serve immediately.

WISDOM HAS BUILT HER HOUSE;

SHE HAS SET UP ITS SEVEN PILLARS. SHE HAS

PREPARED HER MEAT AND MIXED HER WINE;

SHE HAS ALSO SET HER TABLE.

SHE HAS SENT OUT HER SERVANTS, AND SHE CALLS

FROM THE HIGHEST POINT OF THE CITY,

"LET ALL WHO ARE SIMPLE COME TO MY HOUSE!"

TO THOSE WHO HAVE NO SENSE SHE SAYS,

"COME, EAT MY FOOD

AND DRINK THE WINE I HAVE MIXED.

LEAVE YOUR SIMPLE WAYS AND YOU WILL LIVE;

WALK IN THE WAY OF INSIGHT."

Proverbs 9:1-6

Corned Beef with Cabbage, Carrots & Potatoes

MAKES 6-8 SERVINGS

Ingredients

- 5-6 lb corned beef brisket
- 1 tbsp yellow mustard seeds
- 8 allspice berries, slightly crushed
- 2 bay leaves, slightly crushed
- 1 tbsp salt
- 2 tsp ground or cracked black pepper
- 2 cups amber-colored beer
- 2 cups water

- 2 tbsp sugar
- 2 tbsp apple cider vinegar (or white wine vinegar or sherry vinegar)
- 2 yellow onions, peeled and cut into wedges
- 1 lb carrots, peeled and cut into 2" pieces
- 1 lb small red potatoes, cut in half
- 1 head green or napa cabbage, cut into 8 wedges
- 1 cup honey mustard (optional)

Directions

1. Pat corned beef brisket with paper towels, blotting dry. Mix together yellow mustard seeds, salt, pepper, crushed allspice berries and bay leaves. Rub the seasoning mixture all over the brisket. If time permits, chill overnight or a few hours. Remove from refrigerator 30 minutes before cooking to take the chill off.

2. Put seasoned brisket into large pot. Mix together beer, water, sugar, and vinegar and add to the pot. Add onions and about ⅓ of the carrots, and bring to a simmer.

3. Preheat the oven to 300 degrees.

4. Cover the pot with a heat-proof lid and place in oven on center rack. Cook for 3-3½ hours. Remove brisket from pot and place into a large baking dish or sheet pan and cover with foil.

5. Add remaining vegetables to the pot and simmer on the stovetop, covered, until vegetables are tender.

6. Optional Glaze: Heat oven to 450 degrees. Spread honey mustard over top of brisket and roast until top is golden brown and caramelized.

7. To serve, slice brisket thinly, against the grain of the meat, and serve with the vegetables and juices.

Grandma Gardner's Carrot Cake

Ingredients

- 1½ cups corn oil
- 3 eggs
- 2 cups sugar
- 2 cups flour
- 2 teaspoons vanilla
- 2 teaspoons cinnamon
- 2 teaspoons baking soda

- 1 teaspoon salt
- 2 cups shredded carrots
- 1 cup chopped walnuts
- ½ cup crushed pineapple, drained
- 1 cup flaked coconut
- 1 cup raisins

Directions

1. Preheat oven to 350 degrees.

2. Combine corn oil, sugar, eggs, flour, vanilla, cinnamon, baking soda and salt. Stir until all ingredients are nicely mixed together.

3. Stir in carrots, walnuts, pineapple, coconut and raisins. Pour into a greased 13" x 9" pan. Bake for one hour.

GOD SAW ALL THAT HE
HAD MADE, AND IT WAS
VERY GOOD.

Genesis 1:31

April

SHOUT JOYFUL PRAISES TO GOD, ALL THE EARTH!
SING ABOUT THE GLORY OF HIS NAME!
TELL THE WORLD HOW GLORIOUS HE IS!

Psalm 66:1-2

April

At the core of the Christian faith is the cross. Without Christ's death and resurrection, my faith is empty, powerless and, frankly, pathetic. But I believe down to the marrow of my soul that Jesus did come to earth, he did die to redeem sin, and He did raise from the dead and appear to His followers. Now today, over 2,000 years later, "wise men" still seek Him. Wise women do, too.

I AM THE WAY, THE TRUTH, AND THE LIFE.
NO ONE COMES TO THE FATHER EXCEPT THROUGH ME.

John 14:6

Bambino in his Easter Basket, 2014

BE OF GOOD COURAGE AND

HE SHALL STRENGTHEN YOUR HEART,

ALL YOU WHO HOPE IN THE LORD.

Psalm 31:4

Karen Tack, also known as "Cupcake Lady," is a creative genius. Her cookbooks, in collaboration with her partner Alan Richardson are a joy and a delight to look at.

Karen is a frequent guest on *Today* and each time she comes Hoda and I and the entire production staff go crazy waiting to see what miraculous combination of baked goods and candy she's come up with this time. And each time we're more amazed than before.

I wanted her to be a part of *Good Gifts* book because she personifies everything I like in a person: fun, kind, talented, and enthusiastic.

Thank you, Cupcake Lady, for the gorgeous Easter egg cupcakes and "Mom Muffins." You make everything look so easy.

AS FOR GOD, HIS WAY IS PERFECT.
THE WORD OF THE LORD IS FLAWLESS.
HE IS A SHIELD TO ALL WHO TAKE REFUGE IN HIM.

2 Samuel 22:31

GOD IS LOVE, AND HE WHO ABIDES IN LOVE
ABIDES IN GOD, AND GOD IN HIM.

1 John 4:16

Easter Lunch 2014

Andy's Chilean Sea Bass
with orange marmalade sauce
& potato-zucchini pancake

makes 4 servings

Sea Bass Ingredients

- 4 fillets chilean sea bass (6-8 oz ea)
- 2 large eggs
- 1 tbsp salt
- 1 tbsp pepper
- 1 cup all purpose flour
- 3 tbsp unsalted butter

Pancake Ingredients

- 3 large baking potatoes, peeled
- 2 large yellow squash
- 2 large green zucchini
- ¾ cup finely grated parmesan
- 1 tbsp salt
- 1 tbsp ground pepper

Sauce Ingredients

- 1 8oz jar sweet orange marmalade
- ½ naval orange, seeds removed
- 2 tbsp Gold's fresh grated prepared horseradish (hot)

To make Sea Bass:

1. Preheat oven to 350 degrees. Place eggs in a medium bowl and whisk until blended. In a separate bowl, mix together salt, pepper and flour.

2. Heat a large skillet over medium heat. Dip each fillet into egg, shaking off excess, then dredge in flour, coating all sides. Add butter to skillet and once melted add fillets and sauté for 1 minute per side until golden brown.

3. Transfer fillets to a wire rack set over a baking sheet. Place in oven and bake for 12-15 minutes until cooked through. The fish will flake easily once done.

To make Squash-Zucchini Pancakes:

4. Using a sharp knife or Mandolin slicer with straight blade, slice potato, squash and zucchini lengthwise into ¹/₁₆ -⅛" thick slices. Trim the ends of the squash and zucchini so that the length matches that of potato slices.

5. On cookie sheet, assemble each pancake: Place two slices of potatoes side by side; add pinch of salt and pepper and a coating of parmesan cheese. Place 2-3 slices of squash crosswise over the potato slices in an alternate direction, evenly covering potato but not extending over edges. Sprinkle with salt, pepper, and parmesan. Layer 2-3 slices of zucchini crosswise over squash, repeating salt, pepper, and parmesan. Lastly, place 2 potato slices crosswise over zucchini, and sprinkle only salt and pepper.

6. In a 10-12" saute pan over medium heat, add tbsp of olive oil. Slide a large flat spatula completely underneath 1 pancake and carefully transfer to pan. Cook for 3-4 minutes on one side and check underneath for browning. Once golden, turn over and cook until other side is golden and crispy. Transfer to a sheetpan. Repeat for each pancake. If not serving immediately, set aside and re-warm in oven before serving.

To make Marmalade Sauce:

7. Preheat small saucepan over medium low heat. Add marmalade, horseradish and fresh-squeezed juice from orange, stirring frequently until completely incorporated. Once it begins to bubble remove from heat and keep warm.

To serve: On each of 4 large plates, place one vegetable pancake in the center. Top with fillet of sea bass, then a generous drizzle of orange sauce. Serve immediately.

Cassidy's First Easter, 1994

THE LORD YOUR GOD IS WITH YOU, HE IS MIGHTY TO SAVE.
HE WILL TAKE GREAT DELIGHT IN YOU,
HE WILL QUIET YOU WITH HIS LOVE,
HE WILL REJOICE OVER YOU WITH SINGING.

Zephaniah 3:17

*T*his is the season of Resurrection and I adore it. Watching all the dormant landscape come to vibrant life again is always like watching a miracle. *The Chronicles of Narnia* inspired me to write this song with David Friedman for the film of the same name. The producers passed, but I still think it captures the magic of the season.

SPRING

By Kathie Lee Gifford, 2/26/05, Music by David Friedman

INTRO:

From high atop the white-capped mountains

Down to the windswept meadows below

Nature waits at winter's gate

Silently shrouded with snow

From deep within the frozen forest

Across the clouded, white-capped sea

She holds her breath (as she) waits for winter's death

Trembling with expectancy

1. *Something is happening*

    A change is in the air

    You can feel it in your senses

    You can see it everywhere

2. *Yes! Everything is changing*

    Can't you feel it? Can't you see?

    It's there—look at the river!

    It's there—look at the tree!

3. *Listen to the little birds*

    Listen to them sing

    Something wonderful is happening

    How wonderful! It's spring.

4. *Something else is happening*

    Hope is in the breeze

    As the crocuses burst forward

    And the buds burst in the trees

5. *O, how long we've waited!*

    Would winter never leave!

    But now, at last, the winter's past

    O, Narnia, believe!

CHORUS:

Spring, spring! Is anything more glorious?

More welcome, more victorious?

Than spring? Anything?

Can anything compare?

Anytime, anywhere?

To this blessed awakening?

No, nothing is more glorious than spring.

This miracle called spring.

YOU WILL KEEP IN PERFECT PEACE WHOSE MIND
IS STAYED ON YOU. BECAUSE HE TRUSTS IN YOU.

Isaiah 26:3 NKJV

May

THE LORD LOVES RIGHTEOUSNESS AND JUSTICE;
THE EARTH IS FULL OF HIS UNFAILING LOVE.

Psalm 33:5

May

I have lovely Mother's Day memories of growing up and I'm so grateful that my mom is still alive to celebrate the holiday. And since I became a mother myself 24 years ago we have made many special memories together in the Gifford family.

But what do you do when you find yourself without your children at home to mark the day? Invite someone else's child to share it with you! Reed Alexander of the Nickelodeon TV hit, "I Carly" is one of my favorite guest chefs on *Today*. Hoda and I just adore him and have been so impressed by his natural enthusiasm, sweet spirit, and incredible culinary skills.

So it was only natural to ask Reed and his adorable mother, Michele, to join me for a special Mother's Day breakfast. Reed prepared some recipes that were just delicious. Thank you, Reed! Love, your adopted mother!

WISE WORDS BRING MANY BENEFITS,
AND HARD WORK BRINGS REWARDS.

Proverbs 12:14

Reed's Truffle Scrambled Eggs

MAKES 4-6 SERVINGS

Ingredients

- *2 tbsp unsalted butter*
- *12 large eggs*
- *¾ tsp salt*
- *½ tsp ground black pepper*
- *¾ cup whole milk*
- *1 tbsp truffle oil, or to taste*
- *minced chervil, for garnishing*

Directions

1. Slice off the top of the eggs using an egg top remover, placing the eggs into a large mixing bowl. Reserve shells.

2. Rinse the interior of the shells and set aside. Vigorously whisk together eggs, salt, and pepper, until smooth. Add milk to egg mixture and continue whisking until light and frothy.

3. Melt butter in a large, nonstick skillet over medium heat. Add eggs and cook about 8 minutes, until cooked but not tough. Using a nonstick spatula, push cooked egg from the edges of the pan into the interior, stirring occasionally.

4. As the eggs are nearly finished cooking, add truffle oil and gently stir until just combined. Remove from heat and transfer to a plate immediately.

5. To serve, fill eggshells with the scrambled egg mixture and garnish with chervil and additional truffle oil, if desired. Serve in egg cups.

Reed's Maple Brown Sugar Bacon

MAKES 4-6 SERVINGS

Ingredients

- ¾ cup pure, grade-a maple syrup
- ½ cup light brown sugar, packed
- 1 lb low-sodium bacon strips

Directions

1. Preheat oven to 400 degrees.

2. Line a large baking sheet with aluminum foil and place an ovenproof baking rack on it. Set aside.

3. In a saucepan, heat syrup over medium until warm to the touch.

4. Place brown sugar in a small bowl. Pour syrup over brown sugar, and stir lightly to combine.

5. Arrange bacon strips evenly in a single layer, not touching or overlapping, on baking rack. Brush both sides generously with maple-brown sugar mixture. Pour any remaining mixture evenly over the bacon.

6. Bake approximately 25 minutes, or until golden brown and crispy. Remove immediately to a tray or baking sheet lined with paper towel to drain excess fat. Serve while warm.

MAY THE GOD OF HOPE FILL YOU WITH

ALL JOY AND PEACE AS YOU TRUST IN HIM

SO THAT YOU MAY OVERFLOW WITH HOPE

BY THE POWER OF THE HOLY SPIRIT.

Romans 15:13

Reed's Classic Cappuccino

makes 1 serving

Ingredients

- 1-2 shots freshly brewed espresso, regular or decaffeinated (approximately ¼ to ½ cup)
- ⅓ - ½ cup hot, steamed milk
- sweetener or sugar, to taste
- foamed milk, to taste
- ground cinnamon or unsweetened cocoa powder, to garnish (optional)

Directions

1. In a cappuccino serving cup or mug, combine espresso with steamed milk and sweetener or sugar, if using.

2. Garnish with foamed milk and dust with cinnamon or cocoa powder.

3. Serve immediately.

Cinco de Mayo 2014

*M*ay is full of fragrance and color and promise and joy. All at once! It's intoxicating and seductive and seriously glorious. It's almost PERFECT, don't you think? All that magnificence without the stifling heat that we know is just a matter of time.

We take great advantage of Andy and Elvia's gifts during Cinco de Mayo. Mother's Day is always an opportunity to contemplate how much better other mothers seem, isn't it? Another Sunday Brunch to check out if other families seem happier in the restaurant and if other children are better behaved than ours are. But at least it's warmer. And then Memorial Day finally signals the unofficial start of summer. Sadly, we don't spend nearly enough time actually remembering the brave men and women who made the ultimate sacrifice in service to our country. My Daddy served 20 years in the Navy and always expressed his profound love for this country that gave him so much. He lost his stepfather and his brother in WWII and his remaining brother was wounded. But Daddy never focused on the loss. He focused instead on the tremendous privilege it is to be an American. Dear God, we need more men and women and LEADERS like him.

NOW GODLINESS WITH CONTENTMENT IS GREAT GAIN.

FOR WE BROUGHT NOTHING INTO THIS WORLD

AND IT IS CERTAIN WE CAN CARRY NOTHING OUT.

1 Timothy 6:6-7

Fish Tacos with
Chipotle Mayonnaise

MAKES 4-6 SERVINGS

Ingredients

- 1 cup mayonnaise
- 2 tbsp chipotle adobo sauce
- ½ chipotle chili, finely chopped
- canola oil
- 2 pkgs Zatarain's Southern Fish Fry Breading Mix

- 2 lbs Basa or Cod Fish fillets, cut into 2-inch pieces
- 12 corn tortillas
- 4 plum tomatoes, diced
- 2 cups shredded cabbage
- 2 limes, divided into 8 pieces

Directions

1. Combine mayonnaise, chipotle adobo sauce and chipotle chili, and mix thoroughly until completely incorporated. Refrigerate.

2. Pre-heat deep fryer or a deep stock pot filled half way with canola oil to 375 degrees.

3. Place breading mix in a large plastic bag or gallon zip-lock bag. Place fish cubes in bags and shake vigorously until evenly coated.

4. Deep fry for approximately 3 minutes or unitl golden brown.

5. Lay out warmed tortillas and spread an even coat of Chipotle Mayonnaise. Add pieces of fish, a bit of cabbage and tomatoes, and a fresh squeeze of lime. Enjoy!

ANDY'S MARGARITAS

MAKES 1 SERVING

Ingredients

- *1 part (1 oz) fresh squeezed lime juice*
- *1 part (1 oz) quality white tequila (Don Julio is Andy's personal favorite)*
- *1 part (1 oz) agave nectar (Herradura is Andy's personal favorite)*
- *1 part (1oz) water*

Directions

1. Mix lime juice, tequila, agave nectar, and water.

2. Shake and pour over ice in a salted-rim glass.

Elvia's Enchiladas Suisas

MAKES 4-6 SERVINGS

Tomatillo Sauce Ingredients

- 3 lbs small tomatillos
- 2 serano chilis, stem removed
- 5 large garlic cloves, peeled
- 1 white onion, peeled and quartered
- ¼ cup fresh cilantro leaves, stems removed
- ½ tbsp salt
- 2 tbsp Knorr Suiza (chicken flavored boullion)

Enchilada Ingredients

- ¼ cup canola oil
- 18 corn tortillas
- 1 whole roasted chicken, de-boned and shredded
- 2 - 8 oz packages shredded whole milk mozzarella

Directions

To make tomatillo sauce:

1. Fill a large stock pot half way with hot water and bring to a boil.

2. Remove outer layer of tomatillos and place in boiling water. Add serrano chili, garlic cloves and onion and steep for 3-4 minutes.

3. Remove from heat and strain. Reserve ½ cup of stock water (divided between batches) and set aside.

4. Using a food processor or blender, puree all par cooked ingredients in batches, adding stock water to each batch. On the final batch add cilantro leaves, salt, and Knorr Suiza.

5. Once complete, combined all pureed ingredients, mix thoroughly, and set aside. (Can be made and refrigerated in advance and heated prior to use.)

* Excess Tomatillo Sauce makes an great salsa!

To make enchiladas:

6. Preheat oven to 325 degrees.

7. Cover the bottom of an oven proof 13" x 9" casserole dish with approximately 1 cup of tomatillo sauce.

8. In a large skillet, heat oil over medium low heat. Place corn tortillas in oil, flipping twice to coat and soften tortillas.

9. Remove from oil, lay flat, add shredded chicken and mozzarella, and fold into a roll. Place rolls in casserole dish and repeat until filled.

10. Once filled, evenly spread 1 cup of sauce and 1½ cups of cheese over enchiladas and cover with foil.

11. Bake for 12 minutes, then remove foil cover and bake additional 5 minutes, until cheese begins to bubble and toast. Serve immediately.

Sometimes, at the peak of the season, vegetables are so awesome

that all you need is a low flame and a dash of salt.

IF MY PEOPLE WHO ARE CALLED BY MY NAME
WILL HUMBLE THEMSELVES, AND PRAY AND SEEK MY FACE,
AND TURN FROM THEIR WICKED WAYS,
THEN I WILL HEAR FROM HEAVEN, AND WILL
FORGIVE THEIR SIN AND HEAL THEIR LAND.

2 Chronicles 7:14

Memorial Day 2014

June

BY DAY THE LORD DIRECTS HIS LOVE,
AT NIGHT HIS SONG IS WITH ME —
A PRAYER TO THE GOD OF MY LIFE.

Psalm 42:8

June

Now begins the season of serious summer! My heart sings when all the sailboats are settled on their moorings and our beloved harbor comes to life with the sounds of children laughing and splashing and the clanging of the sails against the masts. I sit for hours at Lola's Lookout or Praise Point and just marvel at how it all comes to such a vibrant, happy life.

I CAN DO ALL THINGS
THROUGH HIM
WHO STRENGTHENS ME.

Phillipians 4:13

AS A FATHER HAS COMPASSION FOR HIS CHILDREN,

SO THE LORD HAS COMPASSION FOR THOSE WHO FEAR HIM,

FOR HE KNOWS HOW WE ARE FORMED,

HE REMEMBERS THAT WE ARE DUST.

Psalm 107:28

Frank and Cassidy, Fathers Day 2014

THE LORD DOES NOT LOOK AT
THE THINGS MAN LOOKS AT.
MAN LOOKS AT THE OUTWARD APPEARANACES
BUT THE LORD LOOKS AT THE HEART.

1 Samuel 16:7

CHICKEN PAILLARD
WITH ARUGULA SALAD

MAKES 4 SERVINGS

Chicken Ingredients

- 4 boneless, skinless chicken breasts
- 3 large eggs
- 8 oz finely grated parmesan cheese
- salt and pepper to taste
- Pam non-stick spray

Salad Ingredients

- 2 english cucumbers, julienned into 4" lengths
- 2 large carrots, julienned into 4" lengths
- 4 plum tomatoes, sliced
- italian-style salad dressing, any preferred
- 2 - 11oz packages baby arugula

Directions

1. Butterfly the chicken breasts: Place breast flat onto cutting board so that the pointed end is toward you. Holding the knife parallel to the board, slice through the center of the breast, stopping just before reaching the opposite side. Open the breast, like opening a book, and press the center spine flat. Pound the breast to flatten a bit more and to form one large fillet. Repeat for the remaining 3 breasts.

2. Place eggs in medium mixing bowl and whisk until well blended. Place parmesan cheese in a shallow baking dish.

3. Preheat the oven to 325 degrees. Place a large skillet over medium heat. Dip flattened chicken breast into the beaten egg and shake off excess. Transfer to the parmesan cheese and coat both sides. Season with salt and pepper. Spray skillet with non-stick spray and add 1 chicken breast. Cook for 2-3 minutes on each side until golden brown, then transfer to a baking sheet. Repeat with remaining breasts. Place chicken in oven to keep warm until ready to plate.

Arugula Salad:

4. In a medium mixing bowl place cucumber, carrots and tomatoes. Toss with ¼ cup of dressing and marinate 10 minutes.

5. In another bowl, toss arugula in a light coating of dressing.

To Serve: On each of 4 large plates, place chicken in center. Add a generous mound of tossed Arugula. Top with carrots, cucumber and sliced tomatoes and serve immediately.

THAT YOU MAY WALK WORTHY OF THE LORD,
FULLY PLEASING HIM, BEING FRUITFUL IN EVERY GOOD WORK
AND INCREASING IN THE KNOWLEDGE OF GOD

Colossians 1:10

Cody & Daddy, 1996

I KNOW, OH LORD,

THAT A MAN'S LIFE IS NOT HIS OWN;

IT IS NOT FOR MAN

TO DIRECT HIS STEPS.

Jeremiah 10:23

^ *Phil & Andrea Marella, Joy & Regis,*
and Andrew & Phillip Marella

^ *Regis & Bambino, two of my*
favorite guys in the world!

‹ *The Marellas with special*
guest artist, Kenny Loggins

*O*ne afternoon in 2003, Frank came home from town and told me that Regis & Joy were going to be hosting a benefit that evening for a local family, the Marellas, to raise money to battle a horrendous genetic disease called Niemann-Pick Type C. I had never heard of this disease but when I learned that two of the four Marella children were infected, and the younger daughter, Dana, was Cassidy's age, I knew we had to go. That was Frank's and my first introduction to D.A.R.T—*Dana's Angels Research Trust*—and its founders, Phil and Andrea Marella, and their children Julia, Phillip, Dana, and Andrew. Imagine your beautiful child growing and developing normally until the age of about 5 and then suddenly regressing until they are literally unable to walk or talk or do anything a child normally does. This was the devastating reality this family faced with Dana and her younger brother, Andrew. There is no known cure, although progress is being made every year.

We have been hosting these galas ever since. Dana passed away in July 2013 right before her 20th birthday, and in her honor Frank and I welcomed a special gathering the night before the annual gala at our home. Kenny Loggins, Regis & Joy, and so many faithful friends of Dana and the Marella family and D.A.R.T., came to share their love and memories of her. An angel, indeed. Rest in peace, beautiful girl.

For more information about D.A.R.T, please go to: www.danasangels.org.

Frank, Andrea, Phil, Andrew, Kenny, and Phillip.
I don't think I put Bambino down all night.

LOVE YOUR NEIGHBOR
AS YOU LOVE YOURSELF.
THERE IS NO COMMANDMENT
GREATER THAN THESE.

Mark 12:31

Mom and Daddy under "Eppie's Tree", in the mid-90's.

FOR IN HIM WE LIVE AND MOVE

AND HAVE OUR BEING —

WE ARE HIS OFFSPRING.

Acts 17:28

July

YOUR COMPASSION NEVER FAILS.
THEY ARE NEW EVERY MORNING.
GREAT IS YOUR FAITHFULNESS.

Lamentations 3:22

July

And it's CRAB SEASON! We call our friend, Pete Triantafilos at the Costas Inn in Baltimore, and ask him to ship us a bushel for a feast a couple times all summer. Just spreading out the newspapers on the table fills me with anticipation for my favorite treat in the world. I so remember my Daddy sitting at the picnic table for hours, meticulously picking his beloved crabs and sipping his beer. Then he'd get up to take a break and play some horseshoes, and then start all over again. The smell of Old Bay seasoning still sets me off!

Not too thrilled with the thought of picking a messy crab? Then try Joanie's crab soup and crab cake recipes. Not as much fun, but every bit as delicious.

Little hint: Squeeze lemons on your hands after you pick. Otherwise, you'll smell like a rock at low tide for a week!

Joanie's Crab Cakes

MAKES 4 SERVINGS

Ingredients

- 1 pound <u>lump</u> crab (preferably Maryland Crab)
- 2 eggs, beaten
- ¼ cup chopped onion
- ¼ cup green onion
- dash worcestershire sauce
- ½ cup cracker crumbs
- 3 tbsp mayo
- 1 tbsp prepared mustard

Directions

1. Mix all ingredients together, and form 4 patties. The patties will hold their shape better if refrigerated for 1 hour before cooking.

2. In a large saute pan or skillet, heat 3 tbsp vegetable oil over medium-high until hot. Add patties and cook about 3 minutes per side, until golden brown. Alternately, patties can be cooked under a preheated oven broiler for 3-4 minutes per side, until golden brown.

Joanie's Crab Soup

MAKES 4 SERVINGS

Ingredients

- 1 lb cooked crab or picked crab
- 8 cups water
- 1 large can whole tomatoes
- 1 large onion, chopped
- 3 stalks celery, chopped

- 3 tbsp olive oil
- Old Bay Seasoning
- salt and pepper to taste

Directions

1. Squeeze tomatoes into a juice. Add tomato juice and pulp to large pot; Add water.

2. In a skillet, fry onion and celery until translucent.

3. Add onion and celery to pot with water and tomato mixture. Add salt, pepper and Old Bay Seasoning, to taste

4. Add either 1 pound of cooked crab or a generous amount of picked crab (left over from a feast). Also add crab pieces (with shell) into the pot. *People love picking through these pieces of crab themselves. It also makes the Soup look authentic when served.*

5. Simmer gently until the soup is heated through. DO NOT OVERCOOK!

6. If there is not enough broth SLOWLY add water, but keep tasting; More seasoning may need to be added.

LET US THEN APPROACH THE THRONE OF GRACE
WITH CONFIDENCE, SO THAT WE MAY RECEIVE MERCY
AND FIND GRACE TO HELP US IN OUR TIME OF NEED.

Hebrews 4:16

July 2014

GOD IS OUR REFUGE AND OUR STRENGTH,
AN EVER-PRESENT HELP IN TROUBLE.

Psalm 36:1

Sparklers for the birthday girl!

*I*t seems only right that this special year began with my 60th birthday celebration and it ended with Hoda's 50th here at Gifft Cliff.

Hoda has become a cherished friend and it was wonderful to see her so happy, so full of life, and so excited about the future. She's more beautiful than ever, don't you think? My Egyptian goddess!

Cheers, Hoda Woman!

How many friends does it take to celebrate Hoda's big day? This many!

From the beginning...

... to the end.

It was perfect.

How happy is Frank with his harem?

As we go to print for *Good Gifts* my heart is full of gratitude for all the blessings in my life. Frank and I will be alone again this fall as Cassidy heads off to Texas to film a new movie and Cody heads off to Oxford University in England to begin his Master's Degree in creative writing. While far from perfect, they are both growing into all God has planned them to be and they are finally on their path of potential.

None of us know what the future holds but we all know who holds the future. So we trust in His unfailing love. And I continue to proclaim:

"AS FOR ME AND MY HOUSE, WE WILL SERVE THE LORD."

Joshua 24:15

Acknowledgements

How I wish each person who picks up this book could meet all the special people who made it possible! One of the greatest joys of my life is sharing our home with the people I adore and for whom I am so grateful.

Thank you, Christine Gardner, for organizing everything from A to Z. Meaning, even Zhi Lin! Thank you, Zhi, for driving Bianca to our home for all the photo shoots. Thank you, Bianca Henry, for bringing your gorgeous sense of "style" to our recipes. You are simply the best. Thank you, Gloria Hernandez and Delmina Cisneros, for helping us keep everything clean and on schedule.

Thank you, Brian Doben, for your sense of humor and your incredible photographic eye. Thank you, Andy and Elvia Medina, Reed Alexander, Grandma Gardner, Karen Tack, Joy Bauer, and my family, for your delicious recipes.

Thank you, Christine Dryden, for helping my Christine in putting it all together.

And finally, thank you, Lord, from whom every good and perfect gift comes!

About the Author

Kathie Lee Gifford has enjoyed a five-decade career in the entertainment industry. She is a three-time *Emmy* winner, multiple *New York Times* best-selling author, singer, actress, and playwright.

But her greatest joy is sharing life with her husband, Frank, her children, Cody & Cassidy, and her beloved Lola, Louis, and Bambino at their home in Connecticut.

Other *New York Times* Best Selling books by Kathie Lee Gifford include *I Can't Believe I Said That, Just When I Thought I Dropped My Last Egg,* and *Party Animals.*

Contributors

REED ALEXANDER
Actor, Chef & Author

Reed Alexander is a 19-year-old actor known for his starring roles on Nickelodeon sitcoms such as *iCarly* and *Sam & Cat,* and is the celebrity chef and author behind the hit *KewlBites Cookbook* (Rodale Books, 2013). Today, he can be heard weekly through his lifestyle-centric reports on the very latest food and health news from around the world for the *BBC,* and is presently studying broadcast journalism at New York University. Look for his new cooking show hitting airwaves and followup cookbook hitting shelves soon.

JOY BAUER, MS, RD, CDN
www.nourishsnacks.com

Joy Bauer is one of the world's leading authorities on health and weight loss. As the nutrition and health expert for NBC's *TODAY* show, Joy shares reliable, practical, and easy to follow advice that helps millions of people eat better, live healthier, and lead more fulfilling lives. She also hosts the program's popular "Joy Fit Club" series, which celebrates determined people who have lost more than 100 pounds through diet and exercise alone. She recently released a line of delicious, low-calorie, but nutritious snacks which can be found at nourishsnacks.com.

Profits from the sale of this book will benefit

THE SALVATION ARMY

The Salvation Army has been caring for the hungry, the homeless, the helpless and the hopeless since 1865. I have worked with this extraordinary organization for over 30 years and I am constantly amazed by their devotion to the needy. It is an honor to partner with them in their very special work.

www.salvationarmyusa.org

Editor: Kathie Lee Gifford | Book and Cover Designer: Christine Dryden | Photographer: Brian Doben

Makeup: Edna DeJesus | Hair: Theresa Marra Silicio

ISBN: 978-0-692-26090-6

Printed in the United States of America | 10 9 8 7 6 5 4 3

Published in 2014 by Kathie's Kids, LLC

Old Greenwich, CT

www.kathieleegifford.com